The Supremacy Of Reason: To The Memory Of Maimonides

Achad Ha-Am

The Supremacy of Reason

(TO THE MEMORY OF MAIMONIDES).

AT last, after the lapse of seven hundred years,[1] the anniversary of Maimonides' death has been raised to the dignity of an important national day of memorial, and has been honoured throughout the Diaspora. In earlier centuries our ancestors do not appear to have remembered that so-and-so many hundred years had passed since the death of Maimonides ; still less did they make the anniversary a public event, as we do now, although they were in much closer sympathy with Maimonides than we are—or, to be more correct, *because* they were in much closer sympathy with him than we are. They did not feel it necessary to commemorate the death of one whom in spirit they saw still living among them—one whose advice and instruction they sought every day in all their difficulties of theory and practice, as though he were still in their midst. In those days it was almost impossible for an educated Jew (and most Jews then were educated) to pass a single day without remembering Maimonides : just as it was impossible for him to pass a single day without remembering Zion. In whatever field of study the Jew might be engaged—in *halachah*, in ethics, in religious or philosophical speculation— inevitably he found Maimonides in the place of honour, an authority whose utterances were eagerly conned even by his opponents. And even if a man happened to be no student, at any rate he would say his prayers every day, and finish his morning prayer with the "Thirteen Articles": how then could he forget the man who formulated the Articles of the Jewish religion ?

But how different it is to-day ! If a Jew of that earlier time came to life again, and we wanted to bring home to him as forcibly as possible the distance between ourselves and our ancestors, it would be

---

[1 Maimonides died on the 13th December, 1204. This Essay was first published in 1905.]

enough, I think, to tell him that nowadays one may
spend a great deal of time in reading Hebrew articles
and books without coming across a single reference to
Maimonides. And the reason is not that we have
satisfactory answers to all the spiritual questions
which troubled our ancestors, and have therefore no
need for the out-of-date philosophy of Maimonides.
The reason is that the questions themselves are no
longer on our agenda: because we are told that nowadays
men of enlightenment are concerned not with spiritual
questions, but only with politics and hard, concrete
facts. If Maimonides in his day accepted the dictum
of Aristotle that the sense of touch is a thing to be
ashamed of, we in our day are prone to accept the
dictum that " spirituality " is a thing to be ashamed
of, and nothing is worth notice except what can be
touched and felt. When, therefore, we were reminded
this year that seven hundred years had elapsed since
the death of the man with whom the spiritual life of
our people has been bound up during all the intervening
period, the fact made a profound impression throughout the length and breadth of Jewry. It was as though
our people was quickened by this reminder, and stirred
suddenly to some vague yearning after the past—that
past in which it was still capable (despite all the
Judennot[1]) of looking upwards and seeking answers to
other questions than those of bread and a *Nachtasyl*.[1]

Be that as it may, Maimonides has become the
hero of the moment and a subject of general interest.
Many an address has been delivered, many an article
has been written in his honour this year ; but nobody,
so far as I have seen, has yet used the occasion to
unearth, from beneath that heap of musty metaphysics
which is so foreign to us, the central idea of Maimonides,
and to show how there sprang from this central idea
those views of his on religion and morality, which
produced a long period of unstable equilibrium in
Judaism, and have left a profound impression on the
spiritual development of our people. Since none else
has performed this task, I am minded to try my hand
at it. If even those who are expert in Maimonides'
system find here some new point of view, so much the

---

[1] [Allusion to well-known speeches at Zionist Congresses.]

better ; if not, no harm is done. For my purpose is
not to discover something new, but to rehearse old
facts in an order and a style that seem to me to be
new and to be better adapted to present the subject
intelligibly to modern men, who have not been
brought up on medieval literature.

I.

Can Maimonides claim to be regarded as the
originator of a new system ? This is a question which
has exercised various authors ; but we may leave it to
those who attach importance to names. We may give
Maimonides that title or not : but two facts are beyond
dispute. On the one hand, the fundamental
assumptions on which he built up his system were not
his own, but were borrowed by him almost in their
entirety from the philosophy of Aristotle as presented
at second hand by the Arabs, who introduced into it
a good deal of neo-Platonic doctrine. But, on the
other hand, it is indisputable that Maimonides carried
to their logical conclusion the ethical consequences of
those assumptions, as the Greeks and the Arabs, with
whom the assumptions originated, did not ; and in this
way he did say something that was new and hitherto
unsaid, though it was logically implied in the fundamental principles which he took from other thinkers.

If, then, we would understand the ethical system of
Maimonides, we must set clearly before our minds the
metaphysical assumptions on which it was built.
Those assumptions are so far removed from the
philosophical and scientific conceptions of our own
time that the modern man can scarcely grasp them.
But in those days even the greatest thinkers believed
these airy abstractions to be the solid truths of
philosophy, rock-based on incontestable evidences.
Hence it is not surprising that Maimonides, like the
rest, was convinced beyond doubt that this " scientific "
teaching was the uttermost limit of human understanding, and could never be changed or modified.
So absolute, indeed, was his conviction that he went
so far as to put this teaching in a dogmatic form, as
though it had been a revelation from above.[1]

---

[1] *Mishneh Torah, Foundations of the Law*, chaps. i.-iv.

The following is an outline of his dogmas, so far as is necessary for our purpose :

" All bodies beneath the firmament are compounded of matter and form."[1]   But "form" here is not " form as vulgarly understood, which is *the picture and image of the thing* " ; it is " the natural form," that is to say, the reality of the thing, " that by virtue of which it is what it is," as distinct from other things which are not of its kind.[2]

" Matter is never *perceived* without form, nor form without matter ;   it is man who divides existing bodies in his consciousness, and *knows* that they are compounded of matter and form."[3]   For since the form is the reality, by virtue of which the thing is what it is, it follows that matter without form would be a thing without a real existence of its own : in other words, a mere intellectual abstraction.   And it is superfluous to add that form without matter does not exist in the sublunar world, which consists wholly of " bodies."[4]

" The nature of matter is that form cannot *persist* in it, but it continually divests itself of one form and takes on another."   It is because of this property of matter that things come into being and cease to be, whereas form by its nature does not desire change, and ceases to be only " on account of its connection with matter."   Hence " *generic* forms are all *constant*," though they exist in *individuals which change*, which come and go ; but *individual* forms necessarily perish, since their existence is only possible in combination with finite matter.[5]

" The soul of all flesh is its form," and the body is the matter in which this form clothes itself.   " When, therefore, the body, which is compounded of the elements, is dissolved, the soul perishes, because it

---

[1] *Ibid.*, chap. iv. 2.

[2] *Guide*, Part I., chap. i. [In rendering quotations from the *Moreh Nebuchim* (*Guide for the Perplexed*) the translator has used Dr. Friedländer's English version so far as possible.]

[3] *Foundations of the Law, ibid.,* 7.

[4] In the upper world Aristotle's philosophy postulates the existence of forms divorced from matter : they are the " separate Intelligences," which emanate one from another and are eternal (see *Foundations of the Law, ibid.,* and *Guide,* Part II., chap. iv.).

[5] *Guide,* Part III., chap. viii.

exists only with the body" and has no permanent existence except *generically*, like other forms.[1]

" The soul is one, but it has many different faculties," and therefore philosophers speak of parts of the soul. " By this they do not mean that it is divisible as bodies are ; they merely enumerate its different *faculties*." The parts of the soul, in this sense, are five : the nutritive, the sensitive, the imaginative, the emotional, and the rational. The first four parts are common to man and to other animals, though " each kind of animal has a particular soul " special to itself, which functions in it in a particular way, so that, for instance, the emotion of a man is not like the emotion of an ass. But the essential superiority of the soul of man lies in its possession of the additional fifth part—the rational : this is " that power in man by which he thinks and acquires knowledge and distinguishes between wrong actions and right."[2]

Thus the soul of man differs from the souls of other living things only in the greater variety and higher quality of its functions. In essence it is, like " the soul of all flesh," simply a form associated with matter, having no existence apart from the body. When the body is resolved into its elements the soul also perishes with all its parts, *including the rational*.

This extreme conclusion had already been deduced from the teaching of Aristotle by some of his early commentators (such as Alexander Aphrodisius). There were, indeed, other commentators who, unable to abandon belief in the survival of the soul, tried to explain Aristotle's words in conformity with that belief by excluding the rational part from the " natural form " and attributing to it a separate and eternal existence.[3] But Maimonides was too logical not to see the inconsistency involved in that interpretation ; and so he sided with the extremists, though their view was absolutely opposed to that belief in personal immortality which in his day had come to be generally accepted by Jews. Had he been content with that

---

[1] *Foundations of the Law, ibid.*, 8 and 9.
[2] *Eight Chapters*, chap. i.
[3] See Munk, *Le Guide des Egarés*, I., pp. 304-8 (note).

view alone, he would inevitably have gone back to
the conception of primitive Judaism, as we find it in
the Pentateuch: that immortality belongs not to the
individual, but to the nation ; that the national form
persists for ever, like the generic form in living things,
and the changing individuals are its matter.   In that
case his whole ethical system would have been very
different from what it is.   But Maimonides supple-
mented the teaching of Aristotle by another idea,
which he took from the Arabs ; and this idea, amplified
and completed, he made the basis of his ethical
system, which thereby acquired a new and original
character, distinguished by its fusion of the social and
the individual elements.

The idea is in substance this : that while reason,
which is present in a human being from birth, is only
one of the faculties of the soul, which is a unity of all
its parts and ceases wholly to exist when the body
ceases, yet this faculty is no more than a " potential
faculty," by virtue of which its possessor is able to
apprehend ideas ; and therefore its cessation is inevitable only if it remains throughout its existence
in its original condition—in the condition, that is, of
a " potential faculty" whose potentiality has not been
realised.   But if a human being makes use of this
faculty and attains to the actual apprehension of Ideas,
then his intellect has proceeded from the stage of
potentiality to that of actuality : it has achieved real
existence, which is permanent and indestructible,
like the existence of those Ideas which it has absorbed
into itself and with which it has become one.   Thus
we are to distinguish between the " potential intellect,"
which is given to a human being when he comes into
the world, and is merely a function of the body, and
the "acquired intellect," which a human being wins
for himself by apprehending the Ideas.   This acquired
intellect " is not a function of the body and is really
separate from the body."   Hence it does not cease to
exist with the cessation of the body ; it persists for
ever, like the other " separate Intelligences."[1]

---

[1] *Guide*, Part I., chaps lxx. and lxxii. and *passim*.   For details see Munk
(*ibid.*), and Dr. Scheyer's monograph, *Das Psychologische System des Maimonides*,
Frankfort a /M, 1845.

Now since the form of every existing thing is that individual essence by virtue of which it is what it is and is distinguished from all other existing things, it is clear that the acquired intellect, which gives its possessor immortality, is the essence of the human being who has been privileged to acquire it : in other words, his true form, by which he is distinguished from the rest of mankind. In other men the form is the transient soul given to them at birth ; but in him who has the acquired intellect even the soul itself is only a kind of matter. His essential form is " the higher knowledge," " *the form of the soul,*" which he has won for himself by assimilating " Ideas which are separate from matter."[1]

Thus mankind is divided into two species, the difference between which is greater than that between mankind as a whole and other kinds of animals. For man is distinguished from the rest of animate nature only by having a distinctive form : in quality his form is like the forms of other living things, seeing that in his case as in theirs the individual form perishes. But the distinctive form of the man who has the acquired intellect is distinct in *quality ;* for it persists for ever even after its separation from matter. Its affinity is not with the other forms in the lower world, but with those "separate forms" in the world above.[2]

Thus far Maimonides followed the Arabs. But here the Arab philosophers stopped : they did not probe this idea further, did not carry it to its logical conclusions. Maimonides, on the contrary, refused to stop half-way ; he did not shrink from the extremest consequences of the idea.

First of all, he defined the content and the method of the intellectual process by which man attains to " acquired intellect." If we say that the intellect becomes actual and eternal by comprehending the Ideas and becoming one with them,[3] it follows that

---

[1] *Foundations of the Law,* chap. iv., 8, 9.

[2] There is some ground for thinking that Maimonides thought of the eternal existence after death of the possessors of " acquired intellect " not as personal but as a common existence in which they are all united as a single separate being. See *Guide*. III.. chap. xxvii., and *Foundations. ibid.,* and chap. ii., 5.6. This has been pointed out by Dr. Joel in *Die Religionsphilosophie des Mose ben Maimon,* Breslau, 1876 (p. 25, note).

[3] *Guide,* I., chap. lxviii.

the content of the Ideas themselves must be actual and eternal. For how could something real and eternal be created by the acquisition of something itself unreal or not eternal ? Thus we exclude from the category of Ideas by the apprehension of which the acquired intellect is obtained : (1) those sciences which contain only abstract laws and not the explanation of real things, such as mathematics and logic ; (2) those sciences which teach not what actually exists, but what ought to be done for the achievement of certain objects, such as ethics and æsthetics ; (3) the knowledge of individual forms, which have only a temporary existence in combination with matter, such as the histories of famous men and the like. All knowledge of this kind, though it is useful and in some cases even necessary as preparation, is not in itself capable of making the intellect actual. What, then, are the Ideas by the apprehension of which the intellect does become actual ? They are those whose content is true and eternal Being. This Being includes (going from lower to higher) : (1) the generic forms of all things in the lower world, which are, as we know, constant ; (2) the heavenly bodies, which, though compounded of matter and form, are eternal ; (3) the forms which are free of matter (God and the separate Intelligences).[1] All this relates to the *content* of the intellectual process ; but there is also a very important definition of its *method*—a definition which is implied in the conception itself. The result must be achieved *by the intellect's own activity :* that is to say, man must apprehend the truth of Being by rational proofs, and must not simply accept truth from others by an act of faith. For apprehension by this latter method is purely external ; reason has had no active part in it, and therefore that union of the intellect with its object, which is what makes the intellect actual, is lacking.[2]

---

[1] According to the division of the sciences current in those days, all this knowledge of true Being is contained in Physics and Metaphysics.

[2] All this teaching is scattered up and down Maimonides' works, partly in explicit statements and partly in hints (see, e.g., *Guide*, III. chap. li.). Dr. Scheyer was the first to work out these definitions in detail (*ibid.*, chap. iii.). In general it must be remembered that Maimonides nowhere explains his whole system in logical order, and we are therefore compelled, if we would understand his system as it was conceived in his mind, to make use of scattered utterances, hints, and half-sentences written by the way, to explain obscure statements by others more precise, and to resort freely to inference.

And now let us see what are the ethical consequences of this idea.

The question of the *ultimate* purpose of the universe is for Maimonides an idle question, because it is not within our power to find a satisfactory answer. For whatever purpose we find, it is always possible to ask : What is the purpose of that purpose ? And in the end we are bound to say : " God willed it so," or, " His wisdom decided so."   But at the same time Maimonides agrees with Aristotle and his school that the *proximate* purpose of all that exists in this world of ours is man. For in that " course of genesis and destruction " which goes on in all the genera of existing things we see a kind of striving on the part of matter to attain to the most perfect form possible (" to produce the most perfect being that can be produced ") ; and since " man is the most perfect being formed of matter," it follows that " in this respect it can truly be said that all earthly things exist for man."[1]

Now if man is the proximate purpose of all things on earth, " we are compelled to inquire further, why man exists and what was the purpose of his creation." Maimonides' view of the human soul being what it is, there is, of course, a ready answer to this question.   The purpose of man's existence, like that of all material existence, is " to produce the most perfect being that can be produced " : and what is this most perfect being if not the possessor of the " acquired intellect," who has attained the most perfect form possible to man ?   The purpose of man's life, then, is " to picture the Ideas in his soul."   For " only wisdom can add to his inner strength and raise him from low to high estate ; for he was a man potentially, and has now become a man actually, and man before he thinks and acquires knowledge is esteemed an animal."[2]

But if this is so, can we still ask what is the highest moral duty and what is the most perfect moral good ? Obviously, there is no higher moral duty than this : that man strive to fulfil that purpose for which he was created ; and there is no more perfect moral good than

[1] *Guide*, III., chap. xiii., and Introduction to *Commentary on the Mishnah*, section *Zera'im*.

[2] Introduction cited in last note.

the fulfilment of that purpose. All other human activities are only " to preserve man's existence, to the end that that one activity may be fulfilled."[1]

Here, then, we reach a new moral criterion and a complete " transvaluation of values " as regards human actions in their moral aspect. Every action has a moral value, whether positive or negative, only in so far as it helps or hinders man in his effort to fulfil the purpose of his being—the actualisation of his intellect. " Good " in the moral sense is all that helps to this end ; " evil " is all that hinders. If we determine according to this view the positions of good actions in the ethical scale, we shall find that higher and lower have changed places. At the very top, of course, will stand that one activity which leads direct to the goal—the apprehension of eternal Being by rational proof : that is to say, the study of physics and metaphysics. Below this the scale bifurcates into the two main lines of study and action. In the sphere of study, mathematics and logic have special moral importance, because knowledge of these sciences is a necessary preliminary to the understanding of Being by rational proof. Below them come subjects which have a practical object (ethics, etc.) : for the actions with which these subjects deal are themselves only means to the attainment of the supreme end, and therefore the study of these subjects is but a means to a means.[2] In the sphere of action, again, there are different degrees. Those human actions which have as their object the satisfaction of bodily needs have positive moral value only in a limited sense : in so far as they effectively keep off physical pain and mental distraction, and thus allow a man to give himself untroubled to the pursuit of the Ideas.[3] Above these are actions which are connected with " perfection of character," because that perfection is necessary for the attainment of true wisdom. " For while man pursues after his lusts, and makes feeling master over intellect, and enslaves his reason to his passions, the divine power—

---

[1] *Ibid.*

[2] *Guide*, III., chap. li. Maimonides does not there emphasise the difference between practical studies on the one hand and mathematics and logic on the other, because this is not germane to his purpose at the moment. But the distinction is necessarily implied.

[3] *Guide*, III., chaps. xxvii. and liv. ; *Hilchoth De'oth*, chaps. iii. and iv.

that is, Reason—cannot become his."[1] Hence even
perfection of character has no absolute moral value,
any more than other things which appertain to practical
life. The moral value of everything is determined by
its relation to the fulfilment of the intellectual purpose, and by that alone.[2]

Starting from this standpoint, Maimonides lays
down the principle that virtue is " the mean which is
equidistant from both extremes."[3] This principle is
taken, of course, from Aristotle's doctrine of virtue.
But Aristotle did not set up a higher moral criterion by
reference to which the mean point could be determined
in every case. For him all virtue was really but a code
of good manners to which the polite Greek should con-
form, being enabled by his own good taste to fasten
instinctively on the point equidistant from the ugliness
of the two extremes. Not so Maimonides, the Jew.
He made this principle the basis of morality in the true
sense, because he coupled with it a formulation of the
supreme moral end. This moral end, for which the
virtues are a preparation,[4] compels us and enables
us to distinguish between the extremes and the mean.
For the extremes, being apt to impair physical health
or mental peace, prevent a man from fulfilling his
intellectual function ; the mean is that which helps him
on his road.[5]

But with all this we have not yet a complete answer
to our question about the purpose of the existence of
the human race as a whole. We know that the human
race really consists of two different species : " potential
man " and " actual man." The second species, indeed,
does not come into existence from the start as an independent species, but is produced by development out
of the first. But this development is a very long one,

---

[1] Introduction to *Zera'im*.

[2] Maimonides' attitude to perfection of character is most clearly revealed
by the fact that he calls it " bodily perfection," in contrast to " perfection of the
soul," which is *intellectual* perfection (*Guide*, III., chap. xxvii.).

[3] See *Hilchoth De'oth*, chap. i. ; *Eight Chapters*, chap. iv.

[4] *Guide*, III., chap. liv.

[5] See *Eight Chapters*, end of chap. iv. and beginning of chap. v. Lazarus
(*Ethik des Judentums*, I., chap. xiv.) fails to notice this difference between
Aristotle and Maimonides, and therefore finds it strange that Maimonides intro-
duces Aristotle's doctrine of the mean into Jewish ethics.

and depends on many conditions which are difficult of fulfilment, so that only a few men—sometimes only "one in a generation"—are privileged to complete it, while the great majority of mankind remains always at the stage of "potential man." Thus the question remains : What is the purpose of the existence of the great mass of men "who cannot picture the Idea in their souls" ? For when we say that all material things exist for the sake of the existence of man, we do not mean that all other things are but a "necessary evil," an evil incidental to the production of the desired end— in other words, merely Nature's unsuccessful experi- ments in her struggle towards "the production of the most perfect being that can be produced," like the many imperfect specimens of his art that the inexpert artificer turns out before he succeeds in creating one that is perfect. We cannot so regard them in the face of the evidence that we have of the wonderful wisdom of creative nature, which proves that the Artificer can do his work in the way best fitted to achieve his object. We must therefore assume that "things do not exist for nothing" ; that Nature, in her progress towards the production of the most perfect being, has formed all other things for the benefit of that most perfect being, whether for food or "for his advantage otherwise than by way of food," in such a way that the sum-total of things in the inferior world is not merely a ladder by which to ascend to the production of man, but also a means to secure the permanence of man when once he has been produced. It follows, therefore, that all the millions of men "who cannot picture the Idea in their souls" cannot be void of purpose, like the spoilt creations of the artist, which, not being suited to their object, are left lying about until they perish of them- selves. There must of necessity be some advantage in their existence, as in that of the other kinds of created things. What, then, is this advantage ? The answer is implied in the question. "Potential man," like other earthly things, exists without doubt for the benefit of the "perfect being," of "actual man." In conformity with this view Maimonides lays it down that "these men exist for two reasons. First, to serve the one man (the 'perfect'): for man has many wants, and Methuselah's life were not long enough to learn all the crafts whereof a man has absolute need for his living : and when should he find leisure to learn and to acquire wisdom ? The rest of mankind, therefore, exists to set right those things that are necessary to them in the commonwealth, to the end that the Wise Man may find his needs provided for and that wisdom may spread. And secondly, the man without wisdom exists because the Wise are very few, and therefore the masses were created to make a society for the Wise, that they be not lonely."[1]

Thus the existence of the majority of mankind has a purpose of its own, which is different from that of the existence of the chosen minority. This minority is an end in itself—it is the embodiment of the most perfect form in the inferior world ; whereas the purpose of the majority lies not in its own existence, but in the fact that it creates the conditions necessary to the existence of the minority : it creates, that is, human society with all its cultural possessions (in the material sense), without which it is impossible that wisdom should spread.

Thus we have introduced into ethics a new element—the social element.

For if each man could attain the degree of " actual man " without dependence on the help of human society for the provision of his needs, the moral criterion would be purely individual. Each man would be free to apply for himself the formula at which we arrived above :— all that helps me to fulfil my intellectual function is for me morally good ; all that hinders me is for me morally evil. But if the attainment of the supreme end is possible only for the few, and is possible for them only through the existence of the society of the many, which has for its function the creation of the conditions most favourable to the production of the perfect being : then we are confronted with a new moral criterion, social in character. All that helps towards the perfection of society in the manner required for the fulfilment of its function is morally good ; all that retards this develop-ment is morally evil. This moral criterion is binding for the minority and the majority alike. The majority,

---

[1] Introduction to Zera'im.

whose existence has no purpose beyond their participa-
tion in the work of society, can obviously have no other
moral criterion than the social. But even the minority,
though they are capable of attaining the supreme end,
and have therefore an individualistic moral criterion, are
none the less bound to subordinate themselves to the
social criterion where the two are in conflict. For as
society becomes more perfect, and the material basis is
provided with less expenditure of effort, so much the
greater will be the possibility of producing the perfect
being with more regularity and frequency. Hence from
the point of view of the supreme end of the whole human
race—and that is the source of moral duty—the well-
being of society is more important than that of an
individual man, even though he belong to the perfect
few.[1]

From this point of view all branches of man's work
which further the perfection of society and the lightening
of the burden of life's needs have a moral value, because
they help more or less to create that environment which
is necessary for the realisation of the most perfect form
in the chosen few. Hence, to take one instance,
Maimonides reckons the fine arts among the things that
further the attainment of mankind's end (though
naturally beauty has in his system no independent value):
" for the soul grows weary and the mind is confused by
the constant contemplation of ugly things, just as the
body grows weary in doing heavy work, until it rest and
be refreshed, and then it returns to its normal condition :
so does the soul also need to take thought for the repose
of the senses by contemplating pleasant things until its
weariness is dispelled." Thus " the making of sculptures
and pictures in buildings, vessels, and garments " is not
" wasted work."[2]

To sum up : society stands between the two species
of men and links them together. For the " actual man "
society is a means to the attainment of his end ; for the
" potential man " it is the purpose of his own being.

---

[1] See *Guide*, III., chaps. xxvii., xxxiv. Maimonides is not explicit on the
relation of the minority to social morality ; but his view on this question is
evident from what he says in the chapters quoted, and *passim*.

[2] *Eight Chapters*, chap. v.

The " potential man," then, being in himself but a
transient thing, which comes into being and ceases to be,
like all other living things, must content himself with
the comforting knowledge that his fleeting existence is
after all not wasted, because he is a limb of the social
body which gives birth to the immortal perfect beings,
and his work, in whatever sphere, helps to produce these
perfect beings.

Thus Maimonides gets back to the view of early
Judaism, which made the life of society the purpose of
the life of the individual, although at first he seemed to
diverge widely from it in setting up the one " perfect
man," the possessor of " acquired intellect," as the sole
end of the life of humanity at large.

It is possible, indeed, at first sight to find a certain
resemblance between Maimonides' ethics and another
doctrine which has recently gained such wide currency
—the doctrine of Nietzsche.   Both conceive the purpose
of human existence to lie in the creation of the most
perfect human type ; and both make the majority a tool
of that minority in which the supreme type is realised.
But in fact the two doctrines are essentially different,
and the resemblance is only external.   In the first place,
Nietzsche's Superman is quite unlike Maimonides'
Superman in character.   Nietzsche, Hellenic in spirit,
finds the highest perfection in a perfect harmony of all
bodily and spiritual excellences.   But Maimonides, true
to the spirit of Judaism, concentrates on one central
point, and gives pre-eminence to a spiritual element—
that of intellect.   And secondly, the relation of his
" actual man " to society is different from   that of
Nietzsche's Superman.   The Superman seeks an outlet
for his powers in the world outside him ;   he strives to
embody his will in action, and tolerates no obstacle in
his path.   He is therefore eternally at war with human
society ;   for society puts a limit to his will and sets
obstacles on his path by means of its moral laws, which
have been framed not to suit his individual needs, but
to suit the needs of the majority.   Maimonides' " actual
man," on the contrary, aims not at embodying his will
in the external world, but at perfecting his form in his
inner world.   He demands nothing of society except
that it satisfy his elementary wants, and so leave him

at peace to pursue his inner perfection. He does not
therefore regard society as his enemy. On the contrary,
he sees in society an ally, without whose aid he cannot
attain his end, and whose well-being will secure his own.

II.

So far I have purposely refrained from bringing the
religious element into the ethics of Maimonides, with the
object of showing that he really based his view of human
life on philosophy alone, and did not give way a single
inch in order to effect a compromise between his philosophy and the religious ideas which were accepted by
Jews in his time. None the less, there is no doubt
that Maimonides was a religious man, and believed in
the divinity of the Law of Moses : only his idea of the
nature of religion, its function and its value, was a new
one, and differed entirely from the accepted idea,
because here also, in the sphere of religion itself, he
remained faithful to those fundamental axioms on which
he based his moral system.

Does philosophy leave any room for a belief in the
existence of a revealed religion—that is to say, in a Law
given to men by God through a supernatural revelation
of himself to one or to many individuals ? This question
turns on another : Is the existence of the world
independent of time and external cause, or is it the
result of a creative act of God, as the Pentateuch
teaches ? According to the first view, "everything in the
Universe is the result of fixed laws, Nature does not
change, and there is nothing supernatural." There is
therefore no room for revelation, which upsets the order
of nature, and "the whole teaching of Scripture would
be rejected." But if the world is the result of a creative
act, and nature is consequently nothing but a revelation
of the divine will, made in such time and place as God's
wisdom decreed, then it is no longer impossible that the
divine will should one day reveal itself a second time in a
supernatural manner. Hence, "accepting the Creation,
we find that . . . revelation is possible, and that every
difficulty in this question is removed." For if we ask :
"Why has God inspired a certain person and not
another ? Why has he revealed his Law to one particular nation, and at one particular time ?" and so forth—

" We answer to all these questions : He willed it so ; or, His wisdom decided so. Just as he created the world according to his will, at a certain time, in a certain form, and as we do not understand why his will or his wisdom decided upon that peculiar form, and upon that peculiar time, so we do not know why his will or his wisdom determined any of the things mentioned in the preceding questions."[1]

Maimonides gave much thought to the question of the creation of the world, and examined it from every side. He tried to ascertain whether there was anything conclusive in the evidences adduced by his predecessors in favour of the eternity of the world or of its creation ; and he did not scruple to avow that if he had found a convincing proof of the eternity of the world he would not have rejected it out of respect for the *Torah*. But purely philosophic investigation led him to the conclusion that there was really no convincing proof one way or the other. Seeing then, he says, that " the eternity of the universe has not been demonstrated, there is no need to reject Scripture," and we may believe in the creation theory, which has " the authority of Prophecy," without any sin against our reason.[2]

But when once we have adopted the creation theory, revelation becomes possible, and there is nothing to prevent our holding the belief which our nation has accepted throughout its history : that at a definite point in time the Law was given to our people from heaven through the instrumentality of the chief of the Prophets, who received a unique inspiration from the divine source, and was taught what to tell his people in the name of God.[3] It is not relevant (as we have seen above) to ask why this Law was given to us and not to others, at that

---

[1] *Guide*, II., chap. xxv.

[2] *Guide*, II., chaps. xxv. and xvi.

[3] Maimonides explains his views on the methods of divine revelation and the nature of prophecy in general, and of the prophecy of Moses in particular, in several places : especially in *Guide*, II., chaps. xxxii.-xlviii., and in *Mishneh Torah*, section *Foundations of the Law*, chap. vii. But for our present purpose we need not enter into these speculations. It suffices to say that here also he was true to his own system. The Prophet is for him the most perfect "actual man "; and the divine inspiration reaches the Prophet through that separate Intelligence ("active intellect") which is, according to the philosophical system adopted by Maimonides, charged with the guidance of the world and with the raising of all forms (including the form of the soul) from potentiality to actuality.

particular time and at no other.   But it is relevant to
ask what is the purpose of this Law and what benefit it
was meant to produce.   For it can scarcely be supposed
that God would interfere with the order of nature for no
advantage or object ;   and if we cannot understand the
working of the divine wisdom in every detail, we must
and we can form for ourselves some general conception of
the object for which the divine teaching was given to us
and the way in which it can help men to attain their
end.[1]

Now, it is clear that the divine teaching, whether on
its theoretical or on its practical side, cannot lead a man
straight to his supreme goal—the raising of his intellect
from potentiality to actuality.   For this goal, as we
know, is to be attained not by good actions, and not
even by the *received* knowledge of truth, but only by the
activity of the intellect itself, which must arrive at truth
by the long road of scientific proof.   And if religion
cannot raise its followers to the stage of " actual man "
in a direct way, we must conclude that its whole
purpose is to prepare the instrument which is necessary
for the attainment of that end : to wit, human society,
which creates the environment of the " actual man."
The aim of religion, then, is " to regulate the soul and the
body " of society at large, so as to make it capable of
producing the greatest possible number of " actual
men."   To this end religion must necessarily be popular :
its teachings and prescriptions must be aimed not at the
chosen few, who strive after ultimate perfection, but at
the great mass of society.   To this mass it must give, in
the first place, true opinions in a form suited to the
intelligence of the many ;   secondly, a code of morals,
individual and social, which makes for the health of
society and the prosperity of its members ;   and thirdly,
a code of religious observances intended to educate
the many by keeping these true opinions and moral
duties constantly before their minds.[2]   In these three
ways—the third of which is merely ancillary to
the other two—religion aims at raising the cultural
level of society, so as to make a clear road for

---

[1] See *Guide*, III., xxvi.
[2] *Ibid.*, chaps. xxiii. and xxviii. ; see also II., chaps. xxxiv. and xl.

the perfect individual : to provide him from the beginning of his life with an environment of correct opinions and good morals, and save him from the necessity of frittering away his strength in a twofold battle—against the evil conditions of a corrupt society, and against false opinions implanted in himself by that society. Religion is there to save him from this battle against corruption without and falsehood within : to secure that as soon as he shows the ability and the will to attain perfection he shall find favourable conditions in existence, and proceed towards his goal without let or hindrance.

This was how Maimonides conceived the function of the divine religion ; this was how he was bound to conceive it, his philosophy being what it was. But as he was also persuaded by various reasoned proofs that the Law of Moses was the divine religion,[1] he could obviously have no doubt that this Law must contain on its theoretical side the " true opinions " (that is, those philosophical opinions which he considered true), albeit in popular form, and on its practical side a moral doctrine for the individual and for society which was adapted to the end desiderated by his philosophy, together with the form of religious observance best calculated to educate society in the right opinions and the right morality.

It is at this point that Maimonides' task becomes difficult. Armed with this a priori judgment, he comes to close quarters with the *Torah* : and he finds that in many matters, both of theory and of practice, it is, if taken at its face value, diametrically opposed to what his pre-conceived ideas would lead him to expect. The beliefs embodied in the *Torah* seem to be directly opposed to the most fundamental philosophical truths of Maimonides' system ; the actions prescribed in the *Torah* contain much that it is difficult to reconcile with the social purpose of the divine religion as conceived by that system. What course, then, was open to Maimonides ? To compromise between philosophical and religious truth, as many had done before, was for him impossible. For every com-promise means simply that both sides give way ; and how could Maimonides, with his conviction that the attainment of truth by means of proof is the end of

---

[1] See *Guide*, II., chaps. xxxix. and xl. ; and especially the *Iggereth Teman*.

human existence and the only way to eternal happiness, give up one jot of this truth for the sake of another truth, of inferior value inasmuch as it has come to us only through tradition ? Thus he has but one possible course. Necessity compels him to subdue religion absolutely to the demands of philosophy : in other words, to explain the words of the *Torah* throughout in conformity with the truth of philosophy, and to make the *Torah* fulfil in every part the function which philosophy imposes on it.

This necessity worked wonders. By dint of enormous labour Maimonides discovered various extraordinary ways of interpreting the *Torah* ; with wonderful skill he found support for his interpretations in words and phrases scattered about the Scriptures and the Talmud ; until at last he succeeded in making religion what it had to be according to his belief.

This is not the place to explain Maimonides' methods of exegesis in detail. For us to-day they are but a sort of monument to the weakness of the written word in the face of a living psychological force which demands that " yes " shall become " no " and " no " be turned into " yes." This psychological force led Maimonides to turn the " living God " of the *Torah* into an abstract philosophical conception, empty of all content except a collection of negations ; to make the " Righteous Man " of Judaism a philosopher blessed with " acquired intellect " ; to transform the " future world " of the Talmud into the union of the acquired intellect with the " active intellect " ; to metamorphose the Biblical penalty of " cutting off " into the disappearance of the form when the matter is resolved : and so forth. All this he did in conformity with his " philosophic truth," of which he refused to change one atom.[1]

So, too, with the practical side of religion. Only in a very roundabout way could practical religion be brought under the general principles which Maimonides deduced from his philosophy. The difficulty was especially great in the case of the laws of religious worship, many of which have no apparent educative value as a means of

---

[1] All this is explained in many passages throughout Maimonides' books, which are too numerous to be particularised.

confirming true opinions and morality. But here also
necessity did its work, and Maimonides managed to find
educational " reasons" for all the religious laws, not
excepting those which seem on the face of them actually to
confirm false opinions and to arouse inclinations opposed
to morality—such as, for instance, sacrifices and the
accompanying rites.[1] None the less, he was compelled
after all his hard labour to lay down this strange axiom :
that there is a reason for the commandments in a general
way, but not for their details, these having been ordained
only because there can be no universal without particulars
of some kind or other.[2]

Maimonides had an easier task in bringing the moral
laws of the *Torah* within his system. In themselves these
laws demanded as a rule no heroic exegesis to show
their utility for the social order : indeed, the *Torah* often
emphasises this utility, which in any case is self-evident
in most commandments of this class. But in arranging
these commandments in order of moral value Maimonides was compelled to coerce religion by his characteristic
methods into conformity with his system, according to
which good actions—whether moral or religious—are
of an inferior order, having no value except that of a
necessary preparation of the individual and of society
for the attainment of the supreme moral good, the
perfection of intellect. This attitude of Maimonides
towards moral actions, which we have met already as a
philosophical postulate, is just as strongly maintained after
such actions have been invested with a religious sanctity.
Hence religion affects Maimonides' philosophical ethics
only to this extent, that it makes all the observances
of religious worship a moral duty, equal in value to the
other moral duties, because religious worship is one way
of leading mankind to the attainment of the supreme
moral good in the chosen individuals.

---

[1] For the "reasons of the commandments" see *Guide*, III., chaps.
xxvi.-xlix.

[2] For instance : there is a reason for sacrifices in general. " But we cannot
say why one offering should be a lamb, whilst another is a ram : and why a fixed
number of them should be brought. . . . You ask why must a lamb be
sacrificed and not a ram ? but the same question would be asked, why a ram
had been commanded instead of a lamb, so long as one particular kind is required.
The same is to be said as to the question why were seven lambs sacrificed and not
eight ; the same question might have been asked if there were eight." *Guide*,
III., chap. xxvi.

What, then, is the " divine religion "—that is to say, the teaching of Judaism—according to the system of Maimonides ?

On its theoretical side it is popular metaphysics, and on its practical side social ethics and pædagogics. It cannot bring man to his ultimate perfection ; its whole function is to regulate society—that is, the masses—in accordance with the requirements of the perfect man. Hence religion is not above reason, but below it : just as the masses, for whom religion was made, are below the perfect man. Reason is the supreme judge ; religion is absolutely subordinate to reason, and cannot abrogate one jot of its decisions. For God, who implanted the reasoning faculty in man, that by it he might attain truth and win eternal Being, could not at the same time demand of man that he believe in something opposed to that very truth which is attained by reason, and is the goal of his existence and the summit of his happiness. Even if a Prophet works miracles in heaven and earth, and requires us therefore to believe that there has been prophetically revealed to him some " divine " truth which is opposed to reason, we must not believe him nor " regard his signs." " For reason, which declares his testimony false, is more to be trusted than the eye which sees his signs."[1]

But all this does not detract from the general and eternal duty of observing in practice all the commandments of the divine religion. Religion, like nature, is a creation of God, in which the divine will is embodied in the form of immutable laws. And just as the laws of nature are eternal and universally valid, admitting of no exception, though their usefulness is only general, and " in some individual cases they cause injury as well," so also " the divine guidance contained in the Torah must be absolute and general," and does not suffer change or modification " according to the different conditions of persons and times." For the divine creation is " that which has the absolute perfection possible to its species " ; and that which is absolutely perfect cannot be perfected by change or modification, but only made less perfect.[2]

---

[1] Introduction to Zera‘im.

[2] Guide, II., chap. xxxix., and III., chap. xxxiv.

Religion, it is true, was given through a Prophet, who received the divine inspiration ; but when once it had been given it was placed outside the scope of creation, and became, like Nature after its creation, something independent, with laws which can be investigated and understood by the function of reason, but cannot be changed or abrogated by the function of prophecy. It may happen, indeed, that in accordance with the divine will, which was made an element in the nature of things when nature was created, the Prophet can change the order of the universe in some particular detail for a moment, so as to give a sign of the truth of his prophecy ;[1] and similarly the Prophet can sometimes abrogate temporarily some point of the Law, to meet some special need of the time. But just as the Prophet cannot modify or change completely any law of nature, so he cannot modify or change completely any law of the *Torah*. Nor can he, by his function of prophecy, decide between opposing views on a matter which is capable of different interpretations, because his opinion on a question of this kind is important by virtue of his being a wise man, and not by virtue of his being a Prophet, and it is therefore no more decisive than that of another wise man who is not a Prophet. And "if a thousand Prophets, all equal to Elijah and Elisha, held one view, and a thousand and one wise men held the opposite view, we should have to follow the majority and decide according to the thousand and one wise men and not according to the thousand venerable Prophets." For "God has not permitted us to learn from Prophets, but from wise men of reasoning power and knowledge."[2]

What I have said so far, in this section and the preceding one, is sufficient, I think, to give a clear idea of the fundamental beliefs of Maimonides as to the function of man and his moral and religious duties. But before we pass on to consider how Maimonides tried to make these ideas the common property of his people, and what mark his system has left on the development of Judaism, it is worth while to mention here that Maimonides himself has given us the essence of his system in a per-

---

[1] See *ibid.*, chap. **xxix.** ; *Eight Chapters*, chap. viii.

[2] Introduction to *Zera'im* ; see also *Foundations of the Law*, chaps. ix. and **x.**

fectly unmistakable form, by dividing men into various classes according to their position on the scale of perfection. He compares the striving of man after the perfection of his form to the striving of a king's subjects " to be with the king in his palace " ; and using this simile he finds in mankind six successive stages, as follows :—

1.   Men who are outside the country altogether—that is, savages " who have no religion, neither one based on speculation, nor one received by tradition." They are considered " as speechless animals."

2.   Men " who are in the country," but " have their backs turned towards the king's palace, and their faces in another direction." These are " those who possess religion, belief and thought, but happen to hold false doctrines, which they either adopted in consequence of great mistakes made in their own speculations, or received from others who misled them. Because of these doctrines they recede more and more from the royal palace the more they seem to proceed. These are worse than the first class, and under certain circumstances it may become necessary to slay them, and to extirpate their doctrines, in order that others should not be misled."

3.   " Those who desire to arrive at the palace, and to enter it, but have never yet seen it." These are " the mass of religious people ; the multitude that observe the divine commandments, but are ignorant."

4.   "Those who reach the palace, and go round about in search of the entrance gate." These are " those who believe traditionally in true principles of faith, and learn the practical worship of God, but are not trained in philosophical treatment of the principles of the *Torah*." On the same level with them are those who " are engaged in studying the Mathematical Sciences and Logic."

5.   Those who " have come into the ante-chamber "— that is, " those who undertake to investigate the principles of religion," or those who have " learnt to understand Physics."

6. Those who have reached the highest stage, that of being " with the king in the same palace." These are they " who have mastered Metaphysics — who have succeeded in finding a proof for everything that can be proved — who have a true knowledge of God, so far as true knowledge can be attained, and are near to the truth wherever only an approach to the truth is possible."[1]

In this classification Maimonides sets forth his ethical system in plain terms, with perfect coldness and calm, as though there were nothing startling about it. We of the present day feel our moral sense particularly outraged by his cruel treatment of the second class—" those who happen to hold false doctrines "—though we can understand that a logical thinker like Maimonides, who always went the whole length of his convictions, was bound to draw this conclusion from his philosophical system. For that system regards " true opinions " as something much more than " opinions " : it attributes to them the wonderful power of turning the reasoning faculty into a separate and eternal being, and sees therefore in the opposite opinions a danger to life in the most real sense. But in Maimonides' day the persecution of men for holding false opinions was a common thing (though it was done in the name of religion, not of philosophy) ; and even this piece of philosophic ruthlessness created no stir and aroused no contemporary protest. What did stir contemporary feeling to its depths was another conclusion involved in his classification : namely, " that philosophers who occupy themselves with physics and metaphysics are on a higher plane than men who occupy themselves with the *Torah*."[2] Whoever knows in what esteem our ancestors of that period held the study of the *Torah* will not be surprised that " many wise men and Rabbis " were driven to the conclusion that " this chapter was not written by the Master, or if it was, it should be suppressed, or, best of all, burnt."[3]

Poor, simple men ! They did not see that this chapter could not be either suppressed or burnt except in

---

[1] *Guide*, III., chap. li.
[2] See R. Shem-Tob's Commentary on the *Guide*, *loc. cit.*
[3] *Ibid.*

company with all the other chapters of Maimonides' system, which led him inevitably to this extreme conclusion. But there were other men in Israel who saw more clearly, and actually condemned all the chapters to the fire. To them we shall return later.

III.

The supremacy of Reason ! Can we to-day, after the eighteenth and nineteenth centuries, conceive how tremendous, how fundamental a revolution the phrase implied in the time of Maimonides ?

We all know that the outstanding characteristic of the human mind in the Middle Ages was its negative attitude to human reason, its lack of faith in the power of reason to direct man's life and bring him to the goal of real happiness. Reason was almost hated and despised as a dangerous tempter and seducer : it led men away from the pursuit of truth and goodness, and was to be eschewed by all who cared for their souls. Fundamental questions about life and the universe had to receive *super*natural answers. The simpler and more reasonable the answer, the more suspect and the less satisfactory it was ; the stranger the answer, the more violently opposed to sane reason, the more cordial was its welcome and the more ready its acceptance. The famous *Credo quia impossibile* of one of the Church Fathers was the cardinal rule of thought for all cultured nations, Christian and Mohammedan alike. Nor had Judaism escaped the sway of this principle. Not only the mass of the people, but the leaders and teachers, generally speaking, believed in the literal sense of the Scriptures and the Talmud, even where it was plainly contrary to reason. The coarsest and crudest ideas about the nature of the divine power and its relation to men, and about the soul of man and its future in " the world to come "—ideas which reason cannot tolerate for a moment—were almost universally held ; and even those learned in the Law staunchly maintained these ideas, because so they had found it written in Bible or Talmud, and that which was written was above reason, and no attention should be paid to that impudent scoffer. It followed naturally from this fundamental point of view that the important things in the sphere of morals were to know and to perform all that was written. The function of reason was not to understand life and the universe, but to understand what was written about life and the universe. The thing best worth doing for a Jew was to ponder on the written word and to work out its details, theoretically and practically, to infinity.[1]

No doubt some Jewish teachers before Maimonides had tried to introduce into Judaism more rational principles, which they had derived from Arabic philosophy. But these attempts only affected details; the cardinal principle remained untouched. Reason remained subordinate to the written word; its truths were still discarded for the higher truth of religion. The Gaon Saadiah, the greatest of the earlier Jewish religious philosophers, explains the relation of reason to religion by the following simile. "A man weighs his money, and finds that he has a thousand pieces." He gives different sums to a number of people, and then, " wishing to show them quickly how much he has left, he says that he has five hundred pieces, and offers to prove it by weighing his money. When he weighs the money— which takes little time—and finds that it amounts to five hundred pieces they are bound to believe what he told them." But there may be among them a particularly cautious man, who wants to find the amount left over by the method of calculation—that is, by adding together the various amounts distributed and subtracting their sum from the original amount.[2] Religion, of course, is the weighing process, which gives us the truth at once, by a method which is direct and cannot be questioned. Reason corresponds to calculation : a cautious man with plenty of time may use it to establish a truth which has already been proved to him by the short and certain method of weighing. But obviously calculation cannot change the result which weighing has already given ; and if there is any difference in the results, the weighed money will neither be increased nor diminished, and the

---

[1] Maimonides himself describes the contemporary state of culture among his people in several places. See, for instance, the *Treatise on Resurrection*.

[2] *Emunoth v' Deoth*, Preface.

mistake must be in the calculation. This way of
regarding reason and its relation to religion was common
to all the Jewish thinkers who laboured, before Maimonides, to reconcile religion and philosophy. They regarded their labour only as a necessary evil. They
shouldered the burden because they saw that it had to
be done ; but in their heart of hearts they were wholly
on the side of religion, and it never occurred to them
to give reason precedence.[1]   In this respect they were
like the Arabic religious philosophers ; and like them
they chose the philosophical views which confirmed
their religious faith rather than those which were
confirmed by reason.   "They did not investigate,"
writes Maimonides, jeering at "philosophers" of this
kind, "the real properties of things ; first of all they
considered what must be the properties of the things
which should yield proof for or against a certain creed."
They forgot "that the properties of things cannot adapt
themselves to our opinions, but our opinions must be
adapted to the existing properties."[2]

If we remember that this was the general attitude of
mind, we cannot help asking how it could happen that in
such a period and in such an atmosphere Maimonides
arrived at the doctrine of the supremacy of reason in its
most uncompromising form.   No doubt, if we care to be
satisfied with any answer that comes to hand, we may
say that Maimonides, starting out with a predisposition
in favour of the Arabic version of the Aristotelian
philosophy, and a sternly logical mind, could not stop
half-way, or fail to see the logical consequences of
Aristotelianism.   But when we observe how, with a
devotion far greater than that of his non-Jewish teachers,
he set himself to develop and extend the idea of the
supremacy of reason till it became a complete, all-
embracing theory of life ; and when we remember also his
love for the teachings of Judaism, which ought to have
induced in him a disposition not to extend the empire of
reason, but to restrict it : we are forced to confess that

---

[1] R. Jehudah Halevi, despite his profound knowledge of contemporary
philosophy, says categorically : "He who accepts this [the Law] completely,
without scrutiny or argument, is better off than he who investigates and
analyses " (*Cuzri*, II., xxvi. [Dr. Hirschfeld's translation]).

[2] *Guide*, I., chap. lxxi.

logic alone could never have produced this phenomenon.
There must have been some psychological force, some
inner motive power, to make Maimonides so extreme and
uncompromising a champion of reason.

We shall discover what this motive power was, I
think, if we take account of the political position of the
Jews at that time.

It was a time when religious fanaticism was rife
among the Moslems. In many countries to profess
another religion meant death, and large numbers of
Jews, who could with difficulty change their place of
abode, accepted Mohammedanism, though but out-
wardly. One of these countries was Southern Spain, the
birthplace of Maimonides, who was a boy of thirteen
when religious persecution broke out in that country.
It may or may not be true, as recent historians maintain,
that he and his father and the whole family changed
their religion under compulsion : the question has not
yet been definitely settled. But there is no doubt that
even if he was saved by some means from an open change
of faith, he was at any rate forced to conceal his Judaism,
for fear of oppression, so long as he lived in Spain and
in Fez (where religious persecution first started, and
fanaticism had its stronghold). It was only in Egypt
that his troubles ceased ; and when he reached Egypt
he was already about thirty years of age. This, then,
was the terrible position in which Maimonides spent his
years of development. He was surrounded by lying
and religious hypocrisy ; Judaism had to hide from
the light of day ; its adherents had to wear a mask
whenever they came out of their homes into the open.
And why ? Because Mohammed had called himself a
prophet, had performed miracles, according to his
followers, to win their faith, and by virtue of his pro-
phetic power had promulgated a new Law and revealed
new truths, which all men were bound to believe,
although they were contrary to reason. This state
of things was bound to make a profound impression
on a young man like Maimonides, with his fine nature
and his devotion to truth. He could not but feel every
moment the tragedy of such a life ; and therefore he
could not but become violently opposed to the source
of religious fanaticism—to that blind faith in the truth

of prophecy which relies on supernatural " evidence,"
and despises the evidence of reason. It was this blind
faith that led the Moslems to force the Jews into
accepting the teaching of the new prophet ; and it
was this that led many of these very Jews, after they
had gradually become accustomed to their new situation, to doubt of their Judaism and ask themselves
why they should not be able to believe in Mohammed's
prophecy, just as they believed in that of Moses. If
Moses had performed miracles, then surely Mohammed
might have done the same ; and how could they
decide between the one teaching and the other with
such certainty as to pronounce one true and the other
false ?[1]

These impressions, which were constantly influencing
Maimonides' development in his childhood and youth,
were bound to swing him violently over to the other side,
to the side of reason. Ultimately he was led to subject
man—and God too, if one may say so—to that
supreme ruler : because Judaism could trust reason
never to allow any new prophet with his new teaching to
work it harm. When once Judaism had accepted the
supremacy of reason and handed over to reason the seal
of truth, it would never again be difficult to show by
rational proof that the first divine religion was also
the only divine religion, never to be displaced or altered
till the end of time ; and then, even if ten thousand
prophets like Mohammed came and performed miracles
beyond telling, we should never believe in their new
teaching, because one proof of reason is stronger than all
the proofs of prophecy.[2]

Perhaps, too, Maimonides' rationalism is traceable to
yet another cause, which lies like the first in the situation
of the forced converts of that period. These men were

---

[1] As to the state of mind of the forced converts at that time see what
Maimonides says in the *Treatise of the Sanctification of the Name* and the *Iggereth
Teman.*

[2] See Section II. above. Note especially what Maimonides says about
prophecy in the Introduction to his *Commentary on the Mishnah* (written at the
time when he lived among the forced converts). Some of this is quoted in
Section II. He writes there with such incisive force as to make it clear that he
has left the realm of pure speculation and theory, and has a practical object
connected with actual circumstances which had stirred him deeply at the
time.

no doubt able to observe the Jewish law within their
own homes ; the Moslems did not, like the Christians
later, invent an Inquisition to pry into every hole and
corner. None the less, Maimonides himself makes it
clear that the Jews were often compelled to break the
commandments of their Law, when they could not
observe them without arousing suspicion in the minds
of the authorities. This naturally caused the unfortu-
nate Jews great distress, and drove some of them to
despair. What, they asked themselves, was the use of
remaining true to their ancestral faith at heart, if they
could not in practice keep clear of transgressions both
great and small, and must in any case merit the pains
of hell ? [1] It is reasonable, therefore, to suppose that
this painful feeling also helped to lead Maimonides—
though unconsciously—towards the doctrine of the
supremacy of reason, which teaches that man's " ultimate
perfection does not include any action or good conduct,
but only knowledge " [2]—thus implying that man may
win salvation by attaining to true opinions, though he
is sometimes forced in practice to transgress the
commands of religion.

However that may be, whether for these reasons or
for others, we do find that Maimonides had his system
perfected and arranged in all its details even in his
early days, when he first came out of his study into
public life, and that he made scarcely any change in it
from that time till the day of his death. [3] All his
efforts went to the propagation of his teaching among
his people, and to the endeavour to repair by its means
all the shortcomings which he found in contemporary
Judaism.

These shortcomings were great indeed. Judaism,
as Maimonides found it, was by no means fulfilling its
function as " the divine religion." It was not " true
opinions " that the people derived from Judaism : on
the contrary, they had come, through a literal acceptance

---

[1] All this is clearly hinted in Maimonides' *Treatise of the Sanctification of
the Name.*

[2] *Guide*, III., chap. xxvii.

[3] We find all the principles of his system in the Introduction to his first
book (the *Commentary on the Mishnah*), and again at the end of his last book
(*Guide*, III., chap. li.).

of all that it taught, to hold false ideas about God and
man, and had therefore by its means been removed still
further from perfection. Even the practical duties of
morality and religion could not easily be learnt by the
people generally from their religious writings. For in
order to deduce practice from theory it was necessary
to navigate the great ocean of the Talmud, and to
spend years on minute and tangled controversies—a task
for the few only, not for the masses. Here, then, was
an odd state of things. The whole purpose of religion
was to improve society at large, to speak to the masses
in a language which they understood ; but if the masses
could not understand the language of religion, and
could learn from it neither true opinions nor practical
duties, then religion was not fulfilling its function in
society, and its existence was useless.

This state of affairs produced in Maimonides, while
he was still young, an ardent desire to stand in the
breach and make Judaism fit to fulfil the double function—
theoretical and practical—which it had as the only
" divine religion." For this purpose it was necessary
on the one hand to show the whole people, in a form
suited to its comprehension, the " true opinions "
contained in the *Torah*, and on the other hand to rescue
the practical commandments from the ocean of Tal-
mudic disputation and to teach them in a short and
simple manner, so that they should be easily remembered
and become familiar to the people.

But in those early days Maimonides had not the
courage to strike out a new line and to present the whole
content of religion in an entirely fresh manner in conformity with his philosophical system. Hence he chose
a line which was already familiar, and decided to supply
the need of his own age by the help of a book which in
its time had been intended to fulfil a somewhat similar
purpose—the Mishnah. Thus it was in the form of a
Commentary on the Mishnah that he tried to give his
contemporaries what they lacked : to wit, clear doctrine
and a plain rule of practice. Wherever the Mishnah
leaves a point in doubt, he gives the decision laid down
in the Talmud ; and wherever the Mishnah hints at
some theoretical opinion, he takes advantage of the

opportunity to explain the "true opinions."[1] This latter process was, of course, especially important to him ; and he sometimes expatiates on the subject at much greater length than is usual in a Commentary of the ordinary kind.[2] Thus he was able to introduce into his Commentary, besides a mass of scattered notes, complete essays on questions of faith and philosophy in the form of Introductions to different sections of the Mishnah.[3]

Maimonides gave a great deal of work to this Commentary, which he began and finished in his years of trouble and wandering. In the result he produced a masterpiece, which remains to this day superior to all later Commentaries on the Mishnah. But he did not achieve the principal object for which he took so much trouble : he did not make religion effective. His Commentary did not become widely known, and made no great impression ; still less did it bring about a revolution in popular opinion, as its author hoped that it would. And it failed of its object on the practical as well as on the theoretical side. Many of the later laws, which have no basis in the Mishnah, could not be included in it ; and those that were included were scattered about in no proper order, because the Mishnah itself has no strict order.

But as Maimonides grew older and reached middle life, years brought him wider knowledge and greater confidence in himself. This self-confidence gave him courage and decided him to approach his goal by another road. He would produce a work of striking originality, such as no Jew had ever produced before.

So he set to work on his *Mishneh Torah*. Instead of a Commentary on the Mishnah of R. Jehudah, Maimonides now produced a Mishnah of his own, new in content as

---

[1] See Introduction to *Commentary on the Mishnah*.

[2] "This is not the place to treat of this matter ; but it is my intention, wherever a matter of belief is mentioned, to explain it briefly. For I love to teach nothing so much as one of the principles of religion " (end of *Berachoth*).

[3] Especially important in this connection are the Introductions to *Zera'im*. to chapter *Chelek* (where he brings in all the principles of religion), and to *Aboth* (*Eight Chapters*).

in arrangement.[1]   Here he sets forth all the practical laws of religion and morality and all the " true opinions " in the form best adapted to the understanding of ordinary men, in beautiful and clear language and in perfect logical order. Everything is put in its right place ; decisions are given without hair-splitting arguments ; opinions are set out untrammelled by arguments or proofs. In a word, the book presents all that the divine religion ought to give in order to fulfil its function, and presents it in precisely the right manner.[2]

This time Maimonides was justified in supposing that he had fulfilled his duty to his people and his religion, and had attained the end which he had set before himself. Within a short time this great book spread through the length and breadth of Jewry, and helped considerably not only to make the practical commandments more widely known, but also to purify and transform popular religious notions. Views distinguished by their freedom and their antagonism to current religious ideas appeared here in the innocent guise of canonical dicta ; and as they were couched in the language of the Mishnah and in the familiar terminology of the old religious literature, people did not realise how far they were being carried, but swallowed the new ideas almost without resistance. If the dose was accepted not as pure philosophy, but as religious dogma, that was precisely what Maimonides intended : for according to his system religion was to teach philosophical truth to the masses in the guise of " divine " truth which needed no proof.

---

[1] His Preface makes it clear that he regarded his book as a sort of Mishnah in a new form ; and it seems (though he does not say it in so many words) that he intended to hint at this idea by the title of the book—*Mishnah Torah.*

[2] There were many writers who suspected that Maimonides' idea was to do away altogether with the study of the Talmud. But this suspicion could arise only from failure to understand clearly the real purpose of the book. Even theories are presented here in dogmatic form ; but could it possibly be imagined that Maimonides wanted to do away with the study of philosophy by the long method of argument and proof—that study which he regarded as the purpose of the human race ? The truth is that he had in view the social function of religion, and for this reason he set forth both theories and practical commands in brief and in a mnaner suited to the comprehension of ordinary men. He left it to the chosen few to study the principles of both the theoretical and the practical law, and to obtain from the original sources a knowledge of the reasons for both.

But Maimonides' work was not yet completed. In the *Mishneh Torah* he had reformed religion so far as its social function was concerned : that is to say, so far as the needs of the common people demanded. He had still to reform it from the point of view of the function of society itself : that is to say, to meet the needs of the chosen few. For the common people it was necessary to clothe philosophical truth in religious garb ; for the few it was necessary to do just the reverse—to discover and expose the philosophical truth that lay beneath the religious garb. For this minority, consisting of those whom " human reason had attracted to abide within its sphere "—who had learnt and understood the prevailing philosophy of the time with all its preambles and its proofs—could not help seeing the deep gulf between philosophy and Judaism in its literal acceptation. It was impossible to hide the inner contradiction from such men by means of a superficial gloss, or to harmonise discrepancies of detail by a generalisation. What then should one of these men do if he were not only a philosopher, but also " a religious man who has been trained to believe in the truth of our Law ? " He must always be in a state of " perplexity and anxiety." " If he be guided solely by reason . . . he would consider that he had rejected the fundamental principles of the Law ; . . . and if, instead of following his reason, he abandon its guidance altogether, it would still appear that his religious convictions had caused him loss and injury. For he would then be left with those errors [*i.e.* those derived from a literal interpretation of Scripture], and would be a prey to fear and anxiety, constant grief and great perplexity."[1]

If we remember Maimonides' conception of the " actualisation " of intellect, and how it obtains independent existence through understanding the Ideas, we shall see that he was bound to regard this perplexity of the " perfect individuals " as being in itself not merely something undesirable, but a grave danger from the point of view of the supreme end of mankind. For how could these perplexed men attain to the summit of perfection, to " acquired intellect," if they doubted

---

[1] *Guide*, Introduction.

the truth of reason because it did not square with the truths of religion, with the result that subject and object could not be united in them and become a single, indivisible whole ? If the divine teaching itself brings "loss and injury" to the chosen few, the harm that it does more than outweighs the good that it has done in improving the multitude and thus removing social obstacles from the path of the few.

This grave evil required a remedy ; the "perplexed" had to be satisfied that they could devote themselves peacefully to the acquisition of the Ideas, without being disturbed by the thought that in so doing they were rejecting the fundamental principles of the Law. This was the task which Maimonides set himself in his last book, the *Guide for the Perplexed*. The book is in a way his own confession of faith ; it shows his perplexed pupils the method by which he has succeeded in escaping from his own perplexity. After what has been said above, we need not here deal with this book at length. The "true opinions" which it contains have already been explained in outline ; the method by which these opinions are discovered in the *Torah* has been broadly indicated, and the details are not essential to our present purpose. It does not matter to us *how* Maimonides subordinated religion to reason ; the important thing is that he did subordinate it. From this point of view we may put the whole teaching of the *Guide* in a single sentence. "Follow reason and reason only," he tells the "perplexed," "and explain religion in conformity with reason : for reason is the goal of mankind, and religion is only a means to the end."

Had Maimonides written the *Guide* before he wrote the *Mishneh Torah*, he would certainly have been pronounced a heretic, and his book would have made no deep impression either in the orthodox camp or in that of the doubters. The orthodox would have turned their backs on it and have striven to blot out its memory, as they did with so many other books which they thought dangerous to their faith ; and the doubters would not have accepted its views as a perfect doctrine, but would have regarded it as merely an attempt on the part of one of their fellow-doubters to escape from his perplexity, and an attempt which in many details had failed and could not give entire satisfaction.

But in fact the *Guide* was written after the *Mishneh Torah*, when Maimonides was already considered the greatest exponent of the Law, and enjoyed an un-equalled reputation throughout the Diaspora. Hence even the *Guide* could not dethrone him from his eminence. Willingly or unwillingly, his contemporaries accepted this further gift at his hands. The believers stormed and raged among themselves, but did not dare to attack Maimonides openly so long as he lived. The doubters welcomed the book with open arms ; they did not stop to test or criticise, but drank eagerly of the comforting draught for which their souls had been thirsting. It was not some sophist, but the greatest sage in Israel, the light of the Exile, who went before them like a pillar of fire to illumine their path. How could they but be satisfied with such a guide ?

But things changed when Maimonides' death freed the zealots from the restraint of fear. A fierce conflict broke out about him, and raged for a hundred years. The religious leaders, long accustomed to ban every book that did not suit their views, could not possess their souls in silence when they saw, for the first time in Jewish history, that revolutionary books like the *Guide* and the *Book of Science* were spread abroad without let or hindrance, and were more popular and more esteemed by the people at large than almost any of the other books which the teachers and sages of Israel had placed in the treasury of Judaism.[1] The details of this conflict are familiar to scholars, and it is not my intention here to write the history of that period. But it is worth pointing out that most of Maimonides' opponents at that time did not recognise clearly the fundamental change which he had introduced into Judaism. No doubt they all felt that his teaching meant a complete revolution in the national outlook ; but they did not

---

[1] After the publication of the *Guide* many people discovered that its opinions were already contained in the innocent-looking dicta of the *Mishneh Torah*, especially in its first part (*The Book of Science*), and from that time onward they regarded that book also as heretical, and waged war on it as well as on the *Guide*.

all understand what was the pivotal issue of the revolution. For the most part they merely pointed to certain details in which they found heresy, such as the denial of resurrection, of hell and paradise, and so forth. Only a few of them understood that Maimonides' teaching was revolutionary not because of his attitude on this or that particular question, but because he dethroned religion altogether from the supreme judgment-seat, and put reason in its place : because he made it his basic principle that " whenever a Scripture is contradicted by proof we do not accept the Scripture," but *explain* it in accordance with reason.[1]

This emancipation of reason from its subordination to an external authority is the great and eternal achievement which has so endeared Maimonides to all those of our people who have striven after knowledge and the light. The theoretical system at which Maimonides worked so hard from his youth to the end of his life has long been swept away, together with the Arabic metaphysics on which it was based. But the practical consequence of that system—the emancipation of reason—remains, and has left its mark on the history of Jewish thought up to the present day. Every Jew who has left the old school and traversed the hard and bitter road that leads from blind faith to free reason must have met with Maimonides at the beginning of his journey, and must have found in him a source of strength and support for his first steps, which are the hardest and the most dangerous. This road was traversed not only by Mendelssohn, but also by Spinoza,[2] and before and after them by countless thinkers, many of whom won golden reputations within Judaism or outside it.

S. D. Luzzatto's criticism of Maimonides on the ground that his views on the nature of the soul led to the degradation of reason in Jewish thought is superficial. Maimonides, according to him, " laid down what we must believe and what we must not believe," whereas

---

[1] See the letter of R. Jehudah Alfachar to Kimchi : *Collected Responses of Maimonides* (ed. Leipsic), Part III., p. 1, *et seq.*

[2] See Dr. Joel's monograph, *Spinoza's Theologisch-Politischer Traktat auf seine Quellen geprüft*, Breslau, 1870.

before his time there was no rigid dogma, " and there was no ban on opinions to prevent each thinker from believing what he thought true."[1] Now this is not the place to show how far Luzzatto was from historical accuracy when he credited pre-Maimonidean Judaism with freedom of thought. To understand the true nature of that freedom we need only remember how Maimonides' opponents—who were certainly faithful to the older Judaism—spoke and acted in the period of conflict. But as regards Maimonides himself, Luzzatto overlooks the fact that, while his psychological theory no doubt led him to regard certain opinions as obligatory, he placed the source of the obligation no longer in any external authority, but precisely in human reason. That being so, the obligation could not involve a ban on opinions. For as soon as other thinkers are persuaded that human reason does not make these particular opinions obligatory, they are bound, *in conformity with Maimonides' own system*, to believe each what he thinks true, and not what Maimonides erroneously thought true. In other words : if we wish to judge Maimonides' system from the point of view of its effects on Judaism, we must look not at the Thirteen Articles which he laid down as obligatory principles in accordance with that system, but at the one principle which underlies all others—that of the supremacy of reason. A philosopher who frees reason from authority in general must at the same time free it from his own authority ; he cannot regard any view as obligatory except so long as it is made obligatory by reason. Imagine a man put in prison and given the key : can he be said to have lost his liberty ?[2]

---

[1] See *Kerem Chemed*. III., pp. 67-70.

[2] I may remark in passing that Luzzatto (*ibid.*) accuses Maimonides of yet another disservice to Judaism. By making opinions the essential element of perfection Maimonides, according to him, abolished the difference beween the righteous man and the wicked. " The philosopher," he says, " may commit theft, murder, and adultery. and yet attain eternal life : salvation does not depend on merit." This charge was already brought against Maimonides by his medieval opponents, but it is quite mistaken. Maimonides insists, over and over again, that until a man has moral perfection it is impossible for him to reach intellectual perfection to the degree necessary for the attainment of acquired intellect. See, for instance, the passage from the Introduction to *Zera'im* quoted above (pp. 10, 11).

IV.

Here ends what I wished to say about the supremacy of reason in Maimonides' system ; and here I might conclude this Essay. But I should like to add some remarks on another supremacy——on that of the national sentiment. In these days we cannot discuss the thought of one of our great men, even if there are seven hundred years between him and us, without wanting to know whether and to what extent his thought reveals traces of that sentiment which we now regard as the most vital element in the life of Judaism.

But this question really contains two different questions, which have to be answered differently so far as Maimonides is concerned. The first question is : Did Maimonides recognise the supremacy of the national sentiment in the spiritual life of his people, and allow it consciously and of set purpose an important place in the teaching of Judaism ? The second is : do we find traces of the supremacy of the national sentiment—— as an unconscious and spontaneous instinct—in the mentality of Maimonides himself ?[1]

The first question cannot be answered in the affirmative : the evidence is rather on the negative side. Had Maimonides recognised clearly the strength of the national sentiment as a force in Jewish life, and its importance as a factor in the development of Judaism, he would undoubtedly have used it, as Jehudah Halevi did, to explain the numerous features of Judaism which have their origin in the national sentiment. At any rate, he would not have endeavoured to invest those features with a universalistic character. For instance,

---

[1] Though the conception of "nationalism" in its current sense is modern, the national sentiment itself has existed in our people at all times : and its existence and value have been realised in our literature in every period, from the Bible and the Talmud to the literature of Chassidism, though it used to be called by other names ("the love of Israel," etc.). But the sentiment and its expression do not appear to the same extent or in the same form in all ages and in all individuals, and it is therefore legitimate to ask what was the attitude of any particular age or any particular thinker to the national sentiment. An interesting book might be written on the history of the national sentiment and consciousness in Israel, dealing with their different manifestations in different ages, their growth and decline, and their expression in the life of the nation and the thought of its great men in each period.

in seeking reasons for the commandments he could
easily have found that many of them have no purpose
but to strengthen the feeling of national unity ; and
he would not have said of the Festivals that they
" promote the good feeling that men should have to
each other in their social and political relations."[1]
Nor would he have said, in dealing with the future
redemption, that " the wise men and the prophets
only longed for the days of the Messiah in order that
they might be free to study the *Torah* and its wisdom,
without any oppression or interference, and so might
win eternal life."[2]   No doubt we do sometimes find in
his Letters, and especially in those that were written
to encourage his people in times of national trouble,
feeling references to the fortunes and the mission of the
Jewish people.[3]   But despite these isolated and casual
references, only one conclusion can be drawn from the
general tenour of Maimonides' teaching : that he did
not recognise the value of the national element in
Jewish life, and did not allow that element due weight
in his exposition of Judaism.[4]   On the other hand,
various indications show that in Maimonides himself
the national sentiment was, without his knowledge, a
powerful force : so much so, that it sometimes actually
drove him from the straight road of logic and reason,
and entangled him—of all men—in contradictions which
had no ground or justification in his theory.   We shall
always find in the psychology of even the most logical
thinker, despite his efforts to give to reason the un-
divided empire of his thought, some remote corner to
which its sway cannot extend ; and we shall always
find a rebel band of ideas, which reason cannot control,
breaking out from that point of vantage to disturb
the order of its realm.   Of this truth Maimonides

---

[1] *Guide*, III., chap. xliii. Similarly in chap. xlviii.

[2] End of *Mishneh Torah*.

[3] See the *Iggereth Teman* and the *Treatise of the Sanctification of the Name*.

[4] A German Jewish scholar, Dr. D. Rosin, in his monograph on the ethics
of Maimonides (*Die Ethik des Maimonides*, Breslau, 1876), finds under the heading
of " Nationalism " (p. 148) only two laws in the whole *Mishneh Torah* which
allude to the duties of the Jew to his people. But in fact the two laws which he
quotes (*Hilchoth T'shubah*, chap. iii. 11, and *Hilchoth Matnath 'Aniim*, chap. x. 2)
emphasise rather the unity of the members of one faith.

may serve as an example.   It is particularly evident in
regard to the dogmas of Judaism which he laid down,
accompanied by a declaration that " if any man rejects
one of these fundamental beliefs, he severs himself from
the community and denies a principle of Judaism : he
is called a heretic and an unbeliever, and it is right
to hate him and to destroy him."[1]   As we have already
seen, it is an inevitable consequence of Maimonides'
teaching that the dogmas of religion must be formulated clearly and made obligatory on the whole people.
But in strict accordance with his system Maimonides
ought to have included among the dogmas only those
" true opinions " without which religion could not have
been maintained or have fulfilled its function.   And
in fact all his dogmas are of that character, except
only the two last—those which assert the coming of the
Messiah and the resurrection.   How, then, did he come
to include these two ?

This question was raised soon after Maimonides'
own time (especially in regard to the belief in the
Messiah) ; and his critics rightly pointed out that before
laying down dogmas one must define exactly what is
meant by a dogma, so that we may know how to
distinguish between what may and what may not be
properly so called.[2]   It is indeed strange that Maimonides
forgot so elementary a rule of logic, and still more strange
when we remember that elsewhere, in enumerating the
six hundred and thirteen commandments of the Law,
he was fully alive to the necessity of explaining first of
all " the principles which it is proper to take as a
criterion," in order to select from the multitude of
ordinances in the *Torah* those capital commandments
from which the rest are derived.   For this reason he
fell foul of the earlier enumerations, which he regarded
as ignorantly made and full of mistakes ; and for his own
part he first laid down fourteen " principles," and then
proceeded to enumerate the commandments according to
those principles.[3]   But if this procedure was necessary in

---

[1] Introduction to chapter *Chelek*.

[2] See Albo, *Ikkarim*, Part I, chap. 1.

[3] See his Introduction to the *Sepher Hammizvoth*.

dealing with the practical commandments, surely it was even more necessary in the case of the dogmas of faith. How, then, did it happen that Maimonides embarked on so important a task as the enumeration of dogmas without first laying down some principle by which to guide himself ?

It seems to me that we have to do here not with a casual mistake, but with one of those facts which indicate that the national sentiment was strong enough in Maimonides to conquer even logic. If Maimonides had set out to define the term "dogma" in its purely religious sense, he could not have found the slightest justification for regarding the national belief in a future redemption as a dogma. But he felt that a national hope was necessary to the existence of the nation ; and without the existence of the nation the continuance of its religion is unthinkable. It was this feeling that made him for once oblivious of logic, and prevented him from clearing up in his own mind the nature of religious dogmas in general, so that he might be able to include among them that national belief on which the nation depends for its existence, although it has no direct relation to the maintenance of religion as such.[1]

So also with the belief in resurrection, by which our people has always set great store in its exile. Every individual Jew has suffered the pain of exile not merely in his own person, but as a member of his people ; his indignation and grief have been excited not by his private trouble only, but by the national trouble. He could find personal consolation in the hope of eternity in paradise ; but this did not blunt the edge of the national trouble, which demanded its consolation in the prospect of a bright future for the nation. In those days the individual Jew was no longer, as in ancient times, keenly conscious that successive generations were made one by the organic life of the nation ; and he could not therefore find consolation in the happiness which awaited his people at the end of time, but which he himself would not share.[1] Hence he clung to the belief in resurrection,

---

[1] I remarked on this point years ago in "Past and Future." [See *Selected Essays by Ahad Ha'am*, p. 87.]

which offered what he required—a reward to himself for his individual share of the national grief. Just as every Jew had participated, during his own lifetime, in the national sorrow, so would every Jew be privileged in the future to see with his own eyes the national consolation and redemption. Thus the belief in resurrection was complementary to the belief in the Messiah. United, they gave the people heart and strength to bear the yoke of exile and to battle successfully against a sea of troubles, confident that sooner or later the haven would be reached. When, therefore, Maimonides found it written in the Mishnah (beginning of chapter *Chelek*) that he who denies resurrection forfeits eternal life, he did not feel any need to explain this statement in a sense opposed to its literal meaning, as he usually did when his system demanded it, but took it just as he found it, and made it a dogma. He satisfied his heart at the expense of his head.

Strangely enough, Maimonides himself was perplexed over the question of resurrection, and could not explain why he clung to a belief which it was not easy to combine with his own theory of the soul and the future life. When he formulates the dogmas in his Commentary on the Mishnah, he passes hurriedly over this one, and dismisses it in a few words, as though he were afraid that if he lingered at this point logic would catch him up and ask awkward questions. In the *Mishneh Torah*, again, he does not explain this dogma at all, either at the beginning of the book, where he deals with the Foundations of the Law, or at the end, where he discusses the Messianic Age. This omission led some of his critics to suspect that he did not really believe in a literal resurrection of the body, but explained it in the sense of the immortality of the soul (a subject on which he dwelt very often). This suspicion made him very indignant, and he wrote a whole treatise to prove that he had never intended to take resurrection in any but its literal sense. On the contrary, he maintained that the belief must be accepted literally, and that it was in no way inconsistent with what he had written or with his general view.[1]   But the arguments in this treatise

---

[1] See the *Treatise on Resurrection*.

are all very weak, and the general impression which it leaves is that he did not clearly understand his own mind. He felt instinctively that he could not give up this belief, though it was foreign to his system ; but it was only with great difficulty that he could explain why he allowed it such importance. It was, of course, impossible for a man like Maimonides to admit to himself that he was following feeling rather than reason. He tried therefore to justify his standpoint on rational grounds, but without success.[1]

We find the same struggle between philosophical system and national sentiment in Maimonides' attitude to the Hebrew language. From the point of view of his system he naturally saw no difference between one language and another : what matters is the idea, not its external dress. Hence he lays it down that speech " is not to be forbidden or allowed, loved or despised, according to the language, but according to the subject. That which is lofty may be said in whatever language : that which is mean may not be said in any language."[2] Practising what he preached, he wrote most of his books not in Hebrew, but in Arabic, because he thought that by being written in the ordinary language of his age and his surroundings they would be of greater use from the point of view of their subject-matter. The only book that he wrote in Hebrew was the *Mishneh Torah*; and here also he was guided by practical considerations. He chose the language of the Mishnah because he wanted his people to regard the book with respect as a kind of second Mishnah. The beautiful Mishnaic language would carry off the " true opinions," which needed the help of a sacred language to make them holy and bring them under the ægis of religion. Thus far Maimonides the philosopher. But in his letters we find clear indications that after he had finished his

---

[1] Luzzatto (*ubi supra*) seems to suspect that Maimonides' whole treatment of resurrection was insincere, and that he was deliberately throwing dust in the reader's eyes, in order to conceal his heresy. But this suspicion is absurd : Maimonides was a man who was not afraid openly to reject even the immortality of the soul, and to recast all the fundamental beliefs of Judaism. Any unbiassed reader of the treatise must realise that Maimonides defends resurrection with perfect sincerity, but that he is unable to find the real grounds of his own conviction, because he looks for them in his reason and not in his feelings.

[2] *Commentary on the Mishnah, Aboth,* chap. i. 17.

work his national sentiment proved stronger than his philosophy, and he regretted that he had not written his other works in Hebrew as well. Not only that, but he actually thought of translating them into the national language himself, so as " to separate that which is precious from that which is defiled, and to restore stolen goods to their rightful owner." But the decline of his powers in old age did not permit him to carry out this intention, and the Hebrew translation had to wait for other hands. Some of it was done in his lifetime ; and his letter to the translator of the *Guide* shows how pleased he was.[1]

But there is really no need to look for the influence of the national sentiment in particular parts of Maimonides' work. His work as a whole cannot be fully understood unless we allow for this sentiment. Of course, as we have seen, Maimonides' efforts to improve religion were the result of his philosophy, which taught him that religion must be made fit to fulfil its function in the spheres of theory and practice ; and for his own part he certainly believed that he was actuated solely by this conviction, and was doing, as needs he must, what reason demanded of him. But we, who look at things in the light of modern psychology, which tells us that intellectual conviction is not sufficient to produce sustained effort unless it is accompanied by a strong emotion, whereby the will is roused to conquer all obstacles—we cannot conceive the possibility of arduous work without a compelling emotion. And when we look for the emotion which is most likely to furnish an explanation in this particular case, we shall find none except the national sentiment.

For we know, on the one hand, that religious laws were for Maimonides nothing but an instrument of education—a means of confirming people in true beliefs and good habits of life. Moreover, he regarded many of them (sacrifices and the ceremonial associated with sacrifices) as merely a necessary evil, designed to restrict a bad practice which had taken root in the national life

---

[1] See his letters to Joseph ben Gabar, to the community of Lunel, and to R. Samuel Ibn Tibbon (*Collected Responses of Maimonides* (Leipsic), Part II., pp. 16, 27, 44).

at an early period, and could not be abolished entirely ; and even this justification applied only to the laws as a whole, while their details, as we saw above, were in his opinion wholly without meaning or significance. And yet, holding such views, he worked day and night for ten years to collect all these laws and arrange them, with meticulous exactness, down to their smallest details. Whoever realises the enormous labour that it required to get together the mass of legal prescriptions, scattered over an extensive literature, must admit that no man can be qualified for the work (even if he recognises its usefulness from a certain point of view) unless the work itself has a strong attachment for him. To see the usefulness of the work is not enough ; it must be a real labour of love. What then can have kept Maimonides to his task if not the national sentiment, which made him love his people's Law and ancient customs even where his philosophy did not attach to them any particular importance ?

And on the other side, Maimonides could not have laboured to turn Judaism into a pure philosophy without the help of the national sentiment. We can understand the religious philosopher who tries to effect a compromise between religion and philosophy. The impelling force is his religious feeling : anxious to save religion from the danger threatened by rationalism, he adopts the familiar expedient of dressing religion in the trappings of philosophy, so as to safeguard its essential meaning. But when a philosopher starts, as Maimonides did, with the conviction that there is no room for compromise, but that religion is compelled, willy-nilly, to teach only what reason approves, and when he labours indefatigably to purify religious belief of all supra-rational elements and to turn its essential content into a pure philosophical system, and all this by long and devious methods, which reason cannot always approve : then we are bound to ask what emotion it was that gave him the strength and the will-power required for so difficult a task. Religious emotion certainly gained nothing from a process by which religion was driven from its own throne and deprived of its letters patent as a guide to eternal happiness along a private road of its own. Philosophical emotion—

if the term may be used—might have gained more if Maimonides had accepted and prescribed the method adopted by freethinkers before and after him—that of leaving faith to the believing masses and being satisfied for his own part with reason alone.   But the national sentiment did gain a great deal by the transformation of the Jewish religion—the only national inheritance which had survived to unite our scattered people in exile—into philosophical truth, firmly based on rational and (as Maimonides sincerely believed) irrefragable proofs, and consequently secure for all time against assault.

So we come finally to the conclusion that Maimonides, too, like the other Jewish thinkers, had as the ultimate aim of his great work (though perhaps he did not realise it clearly) the shaping of the content and form of Judaism into a fortress on which the nation could depend for its continuance in exile.   There is only this difference : that whereas his predecessors held Judaism secure because it was *above* reason, Maimonides came and said : "No! Judaism is secure because it *is* reason."

LaVergne, TN USA
18 November 2010
205461LV00010B/13/P